llama llama and me

my book of memories

An Anna Dewdney Book

concept by Reed Duncan

Grosset & Dunlap

An Imprint of Penguin Random House

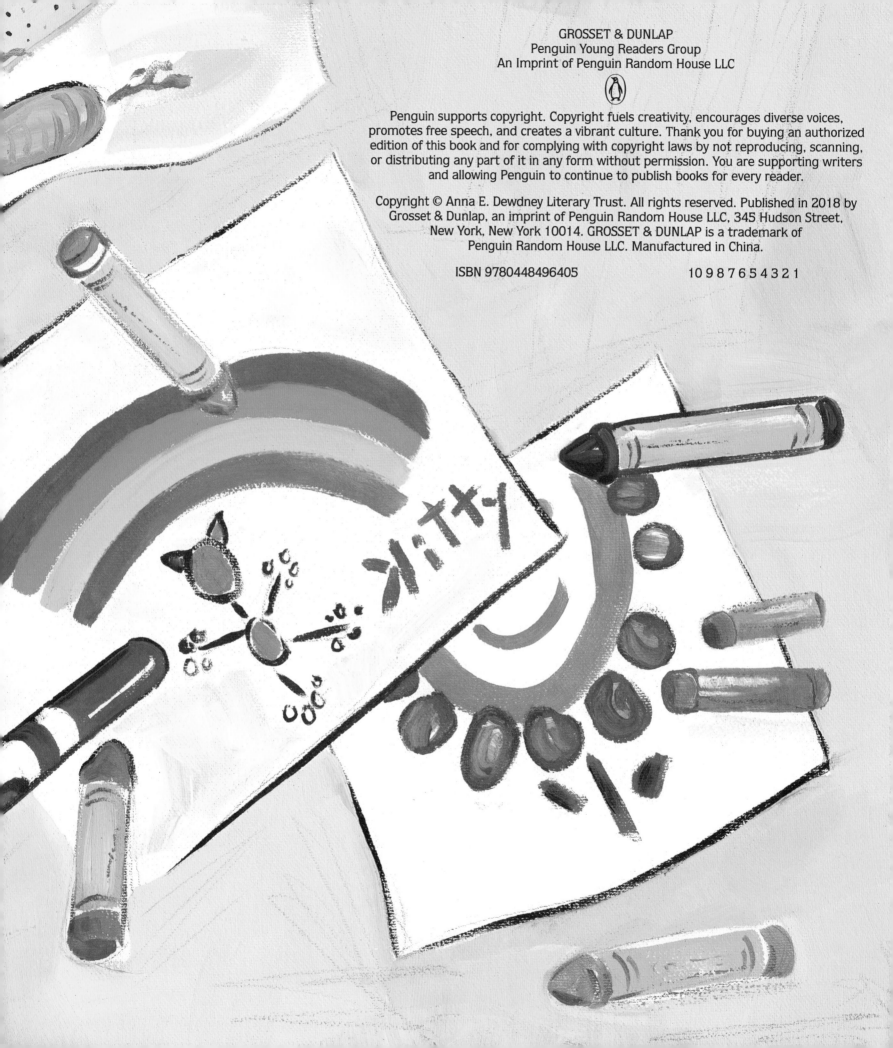

GROSSET & DUNLAP
Penguin Young Readers Group
An Imprint of Penguin Random House LLC

ISBN 9780448496405   10 9 8 7 6 5 4 3 2 1

Put a photo of you as a newborn here.

I was born at 10 o'clock in the
morning / afternoon / evening / **night.**
Circle one.

I weighed 7 pounds and 12 ounces
and was 19 inches long.

Check one:

☐ I wear glasses.

☐ I don't wear glasses.

☐ I wish I wore glasses.

I like the way I look!

Draw yourself here. Use a mirror if it's helpful!

This is my favorite thing about how I look:

....

....

....

....

....

....

....

Llama Llama's family loves him very much.
My family loves me very much, too.
This is my family:

Draw your family in the picture frames, and write their names beneath them!

....

....

....

....

....

Check one:

☑ **I have a pet or pets.**

My pet(s) is/are .....Otis...

☐ **I do not have pets.**

☐ **I want pets! I want a/an** ....

☐ **I do not want pets! I do not want them**
because ....

What is one of your favorite family memories?

....

....

....

....

....

....

This is Llama Llama's family tree.

Grandpa

Gram

Mama

Llama Llama

This is my family tree. It is SO big!

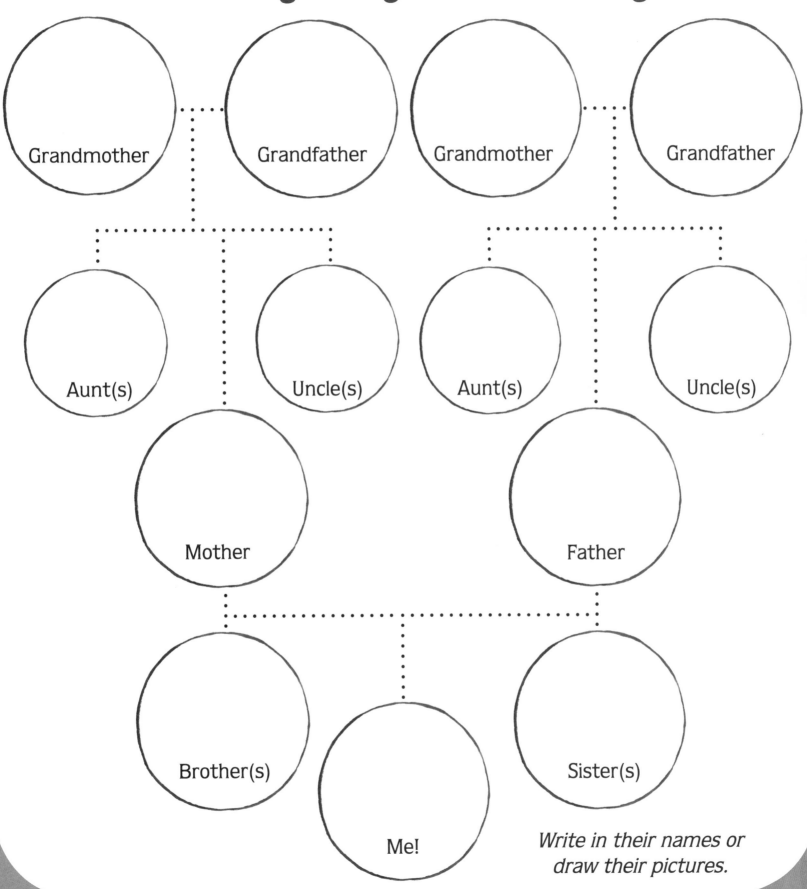

Grandmother

Grandfather

Grandmother

Grandfather

Aunt(s)

Uncle(s)

Aunt(s)

Uncle(s)

Mother

Father

Brother(s)

Sister(s)

Me!

Write in their names or draw their pictures.

I live in .... (city),
.... (state).

This is what my house looks like:

Draw your house or apartment building here.

These are my neighbors:

Draw your neighbors, and write their names beneath them.

My bedroom is MY special place.
This is what my bedroom looks like:

Draw your bedroom here.

My bedroom is (neat/messy).

My favorite thing about my bedroom is

....

This is how I get ready for bed every night:

....

....

....

....

Do you remember any of your dreams? Write one down here!

....

....

....

I have a GREAT personality!

I am:

Circle the words that describe you.

funny

silly

serious

kind

brave

shy

friendly

talkative

unique

curious

artistic

What is a funny story about your personality?

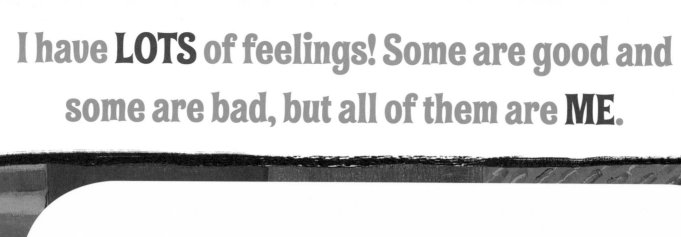

I have **LOTS** of feelings! Some are good and some are bad, but all of them are **ME**.

This is a time I felt happy:

....

....

....

....

....

....

....

....

....

This is a time I felt sad:

....

....

....

....

This is a time I felt brave:

....

....

....

....

This is a time I felt silly:

....

....

....

....

This is a time I felt mad:

....

....

....

....

This is a time I did not want to share:

....

....

....

....

This is a time I laughed a lot:

....

....

....

....

Llama Llama's best friend is Nelly Gnu. My best friend is really nice. My best friend's name is..

Put a photo or draw a picture of your best friend here.

I like my best friend because

....

....

....

....

I have a lot of special memories with my best friend. Here is my favorite:

....

....

....

....

Llama's other friends are Euclid, Gilroy, and Luna. I have other friends, too. They are

....

When I am with my friends, we like to

....

....

....

....

....

Put photos of your friends here, or draw them instead.

I am a VERY good friend. I think a good friend . . .

Circle the words you agree with, and write down some ideas of your own.

is kind to others

shares toys

tells jokes

gives help when
it is needed

likes to have fun

is a good listener

can keep a secret

tells the truth

is happy to see you

**likes spending time
with you**

....

....

....

....

The name of my school is ....

This is what my school looks like:

Draw your school here.

My teacher's name is ....

My favorite subject is ....

I like learning about ....

What do you remember about your first day of school?

....

....

....

....

....

My favorite thing about school is

My least favorite thing about school is

Once, I had to stay home from school because

I was sick with ....

I felt ....

....

....

....

How did you spend your sick day?

....

....

....

....

....

....

....

....

....

....

I like to:

Check one:

- ☐ **read**
- ☐ draw
- ☐ paint
- ☐ write
- ☐ **sing**
- ☐ **listen to music**
- ☐ cook
- ☐ play board games
- ☐ solve puzzles
- ☐ dance
- ☐ **run**
- ☐ play sports
- ☐ play on the playground

Llama Llama's stuffed animal is Fuzzy Llama. My favorite stuffed animal is ....

Draw your favorite stuffed animal here.

This is how I got my stuffed animal:

....

....

....

....

....

....

....

....

....

My favorite color is...

My favorite season is...

My favorite place is ....

My favorite song is ....

My favorite book is ....

My favorite game is ....

My favorite sport is ....

My favorite TV show is...

My favorite movie is ....

My favorite food is .... *YUM!*

Draw your favorite food here.

My least favorite food is .... *YUCK!*

Draw your least favorite food here.

My favorite holiday is .... **because**

....

....

....

....

....

....

....

What is one of your favorite holiday memories?

....

....

....

....

....

Put a photo or draw a picture of a holiday memory here.

I like to go to new places!
These are some of the places I have visited:

*Fill in the postcards with the names and drawings
or photos of places you've been.*

Here's what happened when I went somewhere new:

....

....

....

....

....

....

Someday I would like to travel to:

....

....

....

....

....

....

....

....

....

When I grow up, I would like to be a/an ....,

or a/an ....,

or a/an ....

I think these jobs sound like fun!

Circle the jobs you think sound interesting.

astronaut	writer	police officer
doctor	scientist	president
comedian	computer programmer	....
nurse		....
musician	lawyer	....
pilot	artist	....
teacher	businessperson	....
mathematician	firefighter	....

How do you picture yourself as a grown-up?

Draw grown-up YOU here!

Whew! I'm all done.

I finished this book on _____ (date)
with the help of _____.
Here is a drawing of us together.